Book Corner

Emily Snowdon

For my grandmother,

who filled my life with fairytales,
magic and, most importantly,
taught me to paint.
I wouldn't be an artist without you.

THIS BOOK BELONGS TO

BEFORE YOU START COLOURING

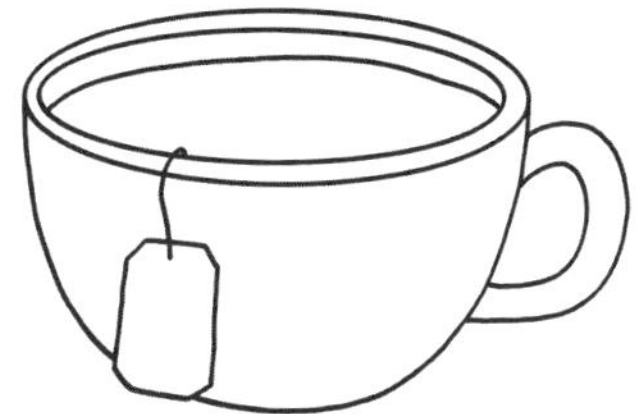

Welcome to your bookish colouring happy place!

Made with love, these illustrations were designed to be personalised, so the spines of books have been left deliberately blank for you to add your favourite titles.

For the best colouring experience, I recommend finding a cosy nook of your own and curling up with your favourite beverage or snack. I'd also suggest placing a thick piece of card behind the page you're colouring to protect the next illustration.

A world of cosy colouring awaits . . .

TEST COLOUR PAGE

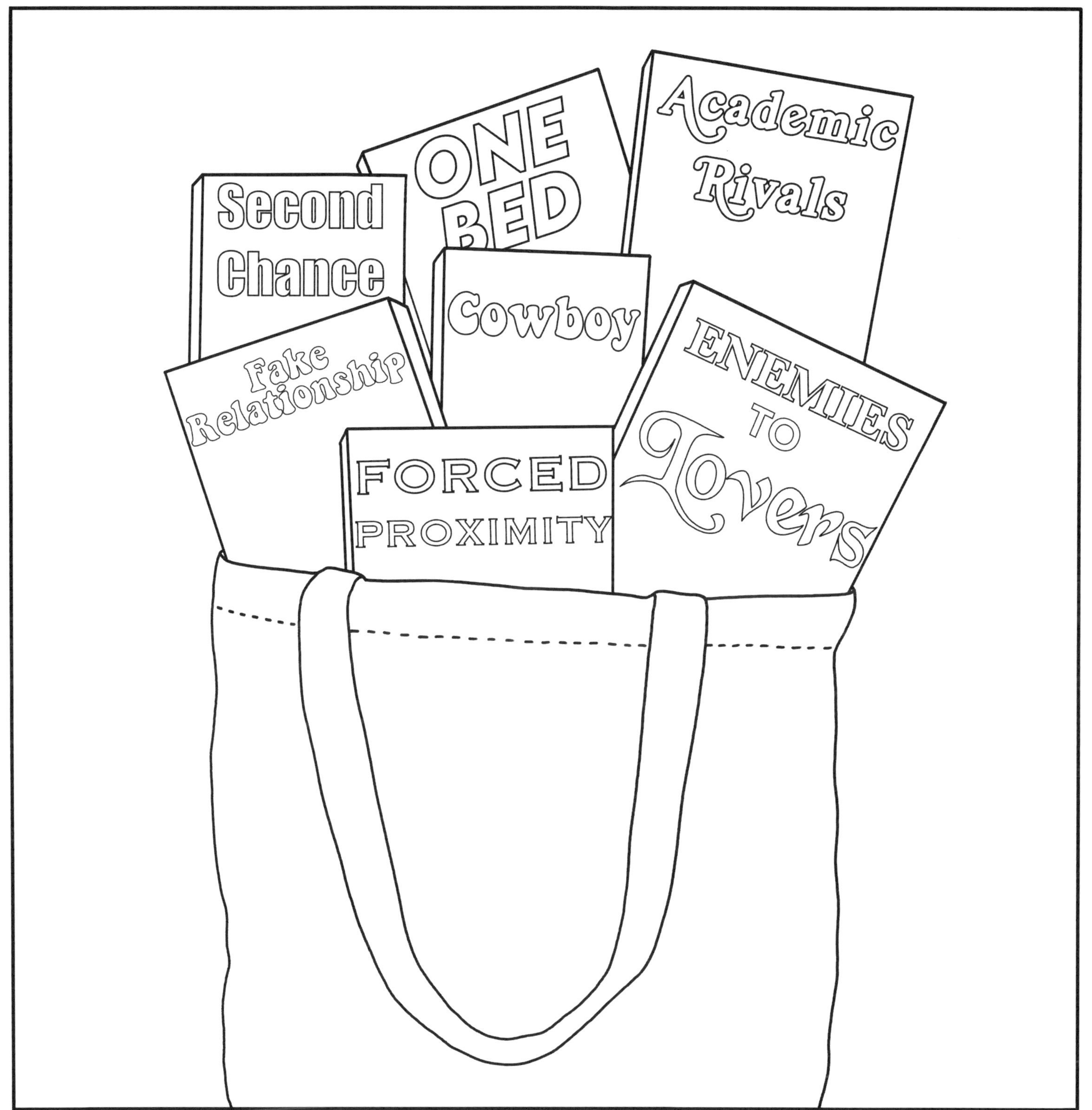
Second Chance
ONE BED
Academic Rivals
Fake Relationship
Cowboy
ENEMIES TO Lovers
FORCED PROXIMITY

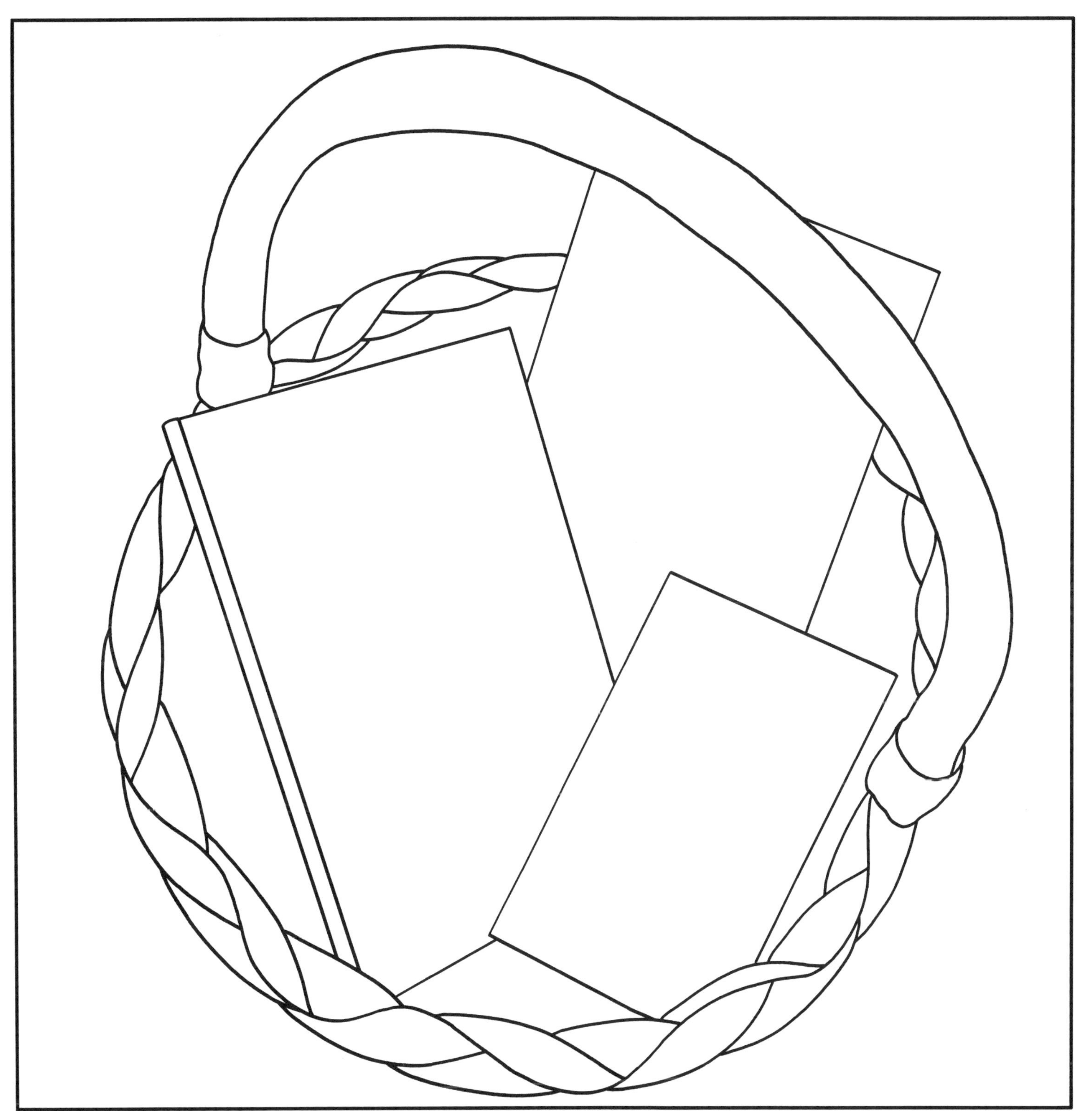

STAR CROSSED LOVERS
ACADEMI IVALS
SECOND ANCE
ONE BED
ENEMIES to LOVERS
FAKE RELATIONSHIP

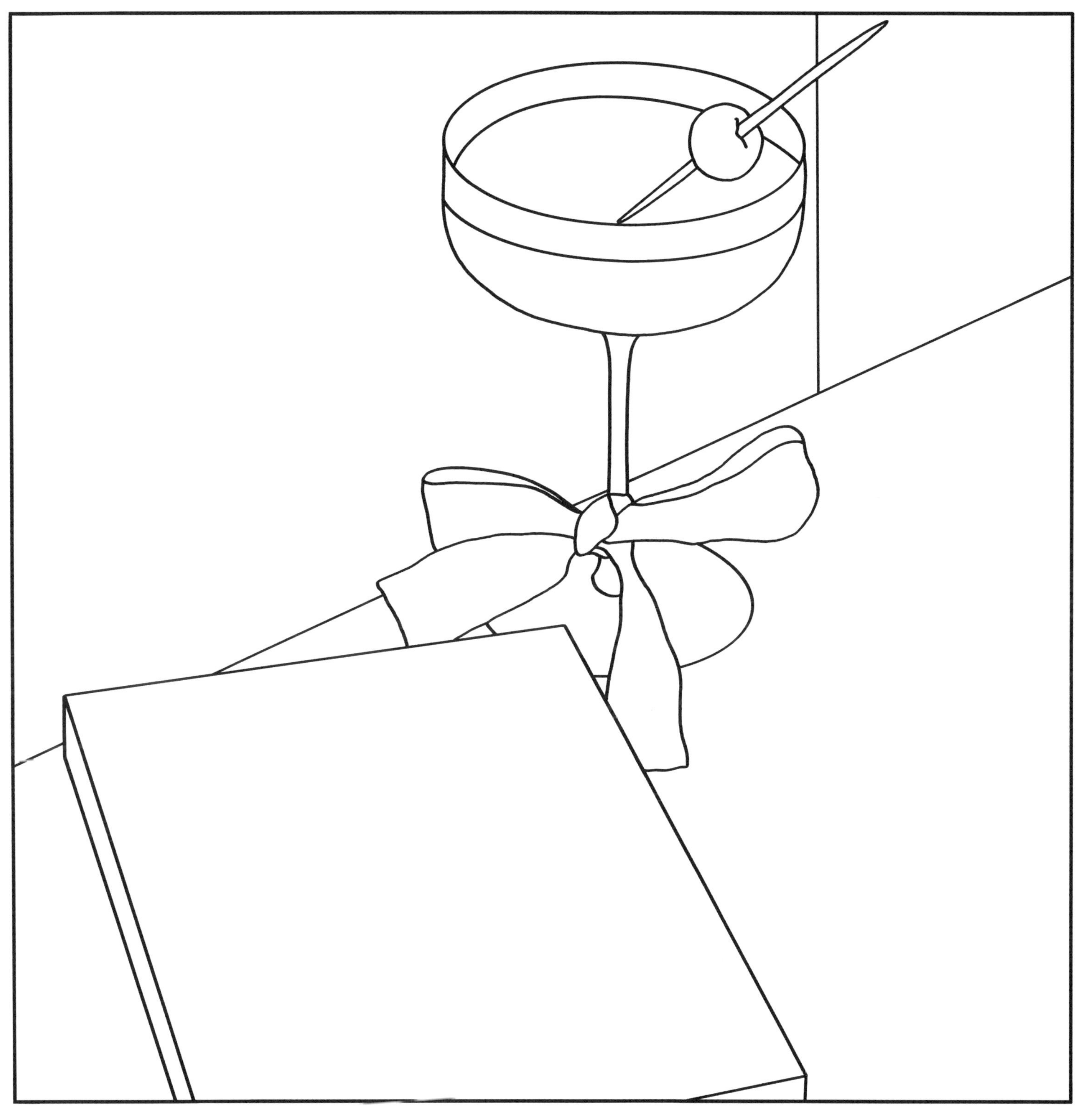

The chosen one
DARK FAMILY SECRET
THE QUEST

Star Crossed
Lovers

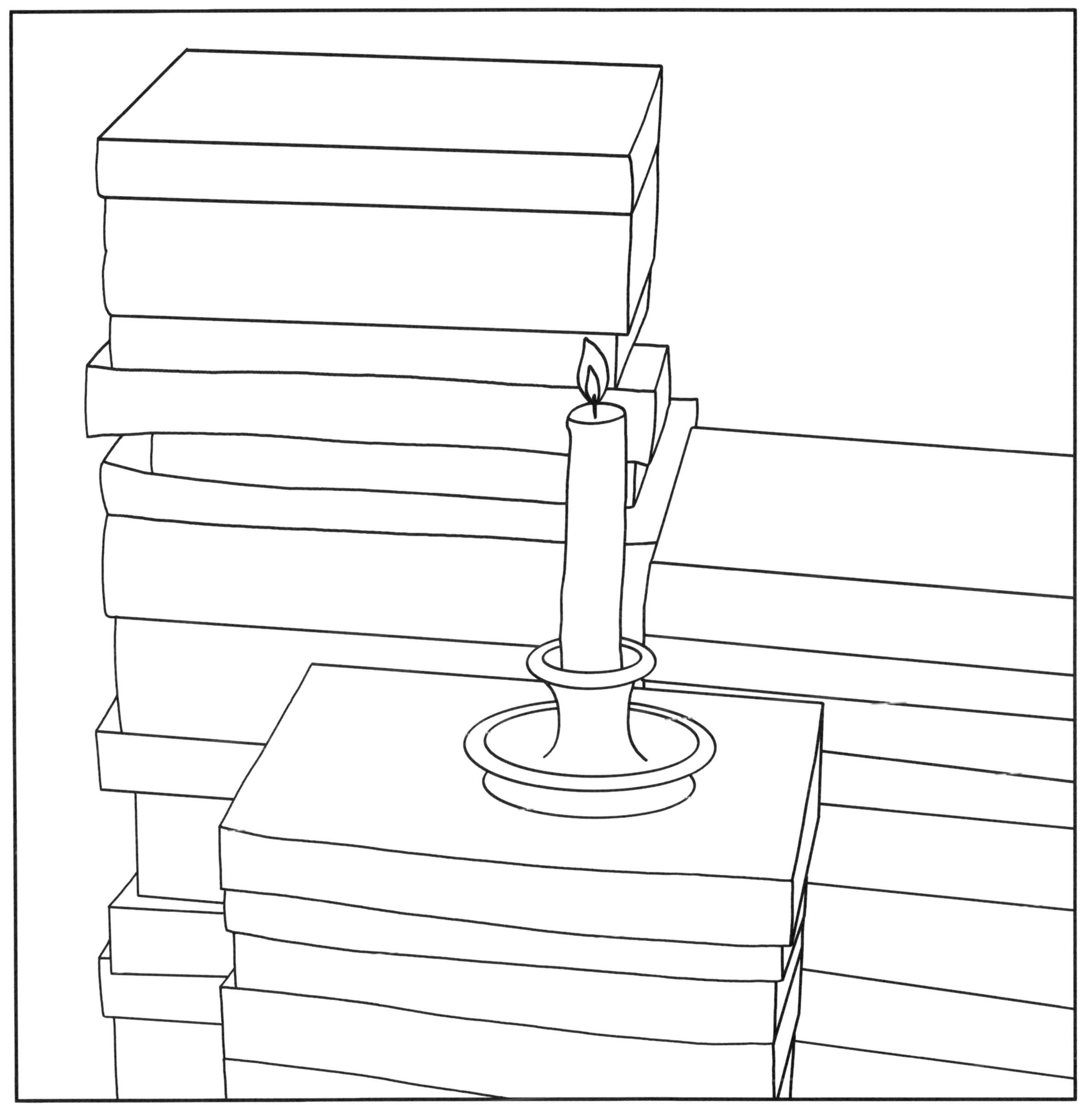

Academic
Rivals

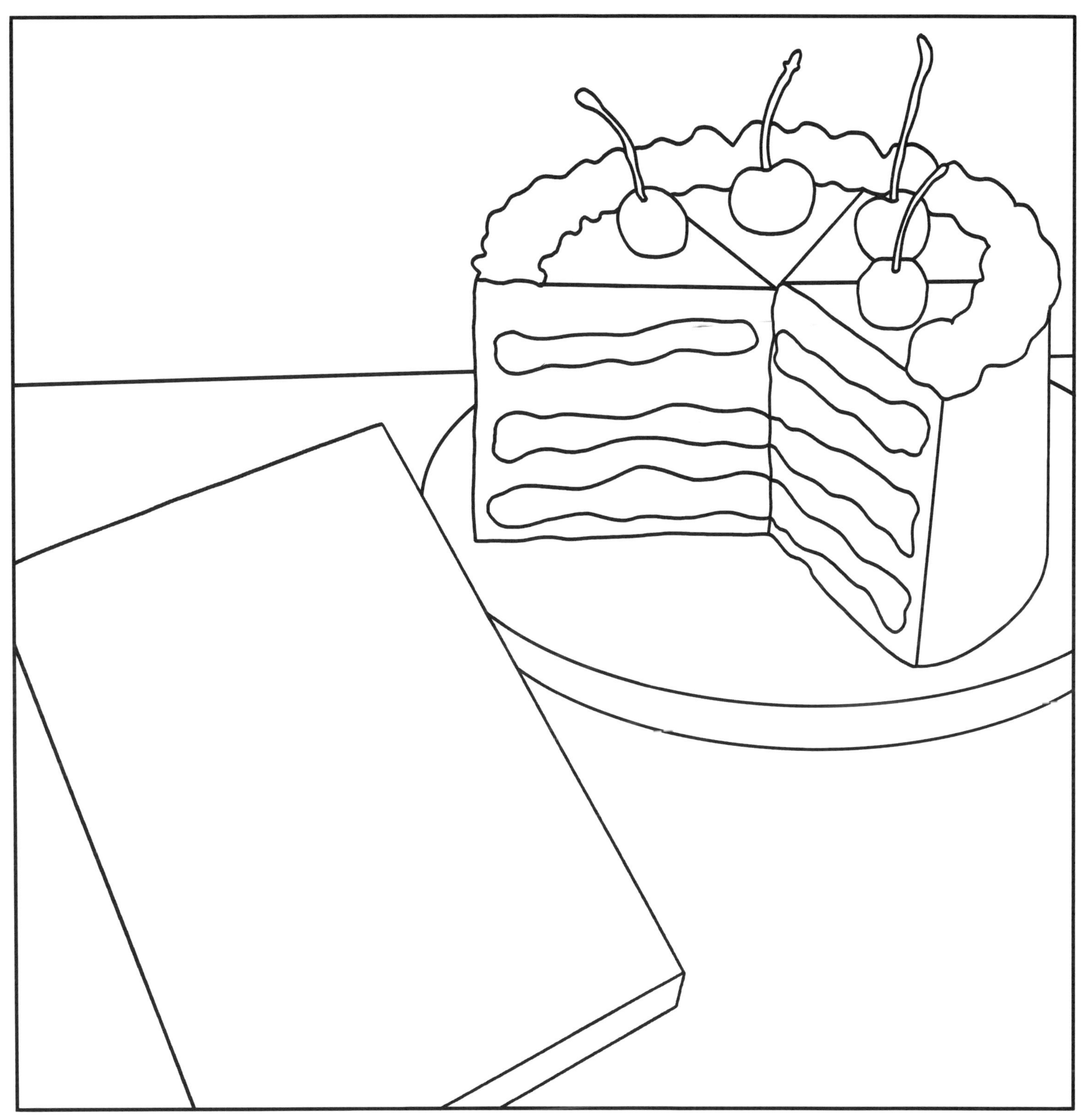

ENEMIES
TO
Lovers
FORCED
PROXIMITY

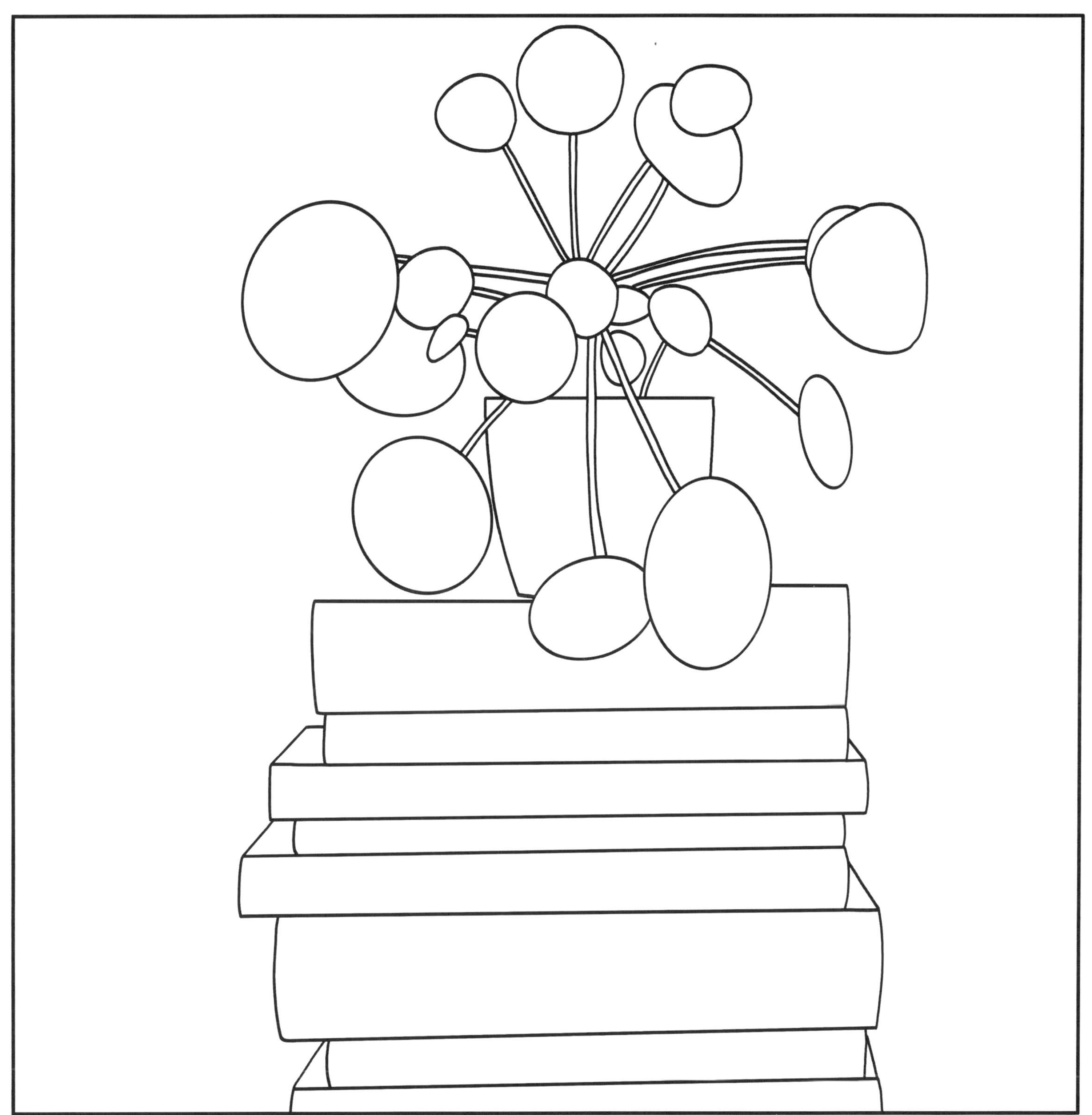

ABOUT THE AUTHOR

Emily is a fulltime social worker with a lifelong artistic streak. During the pandemic, she poured herself into her art and grew a community of fans through her signature tablescapes and bookish artworks.

Several years on, Emily's art prints, original paintings, collaborations and custom commissions adorn homes and businesses across Australia and around the world.

She loves the therapeutic nature of art and particularly enjoys capturing the simple moments in life. With vibrant colours and rich textures, she demonstrates how everyday objects such as food, table settings and book stacks evoke beauty and nostalgia.

Emily is excited to share her love of reading by encouraging others to put their own creative spin on these cosy bookish scenes.

emily.snowdon.artist

www.emilysnowdonartist.com

PENGUIN BOOKS

UK | USA | Canada | Ireland | Australia
India | New Zealand | South Africa | China

Penguin Books is part of the Penguin Random House group of companies
whose addresses can be found at global.penguinrandomhouse.com

First published by Penguin Books in 2026

Cover and internal illustrations by Emily Snowdon
Cover design by Adam Laszczuk © Penguin Random House Australia Pty Ltd
Internal design by Adam Laszczuk

Printed and bound in Australia by Griffin Press, an accredited
ISO AS/NZS 14001 Environmental Management Systems printer

A catalogue record for this book is available from the National Library of Australia

ISBN 978 1 76135 935 4

penguin.com.au

We at Penguin Random House Australia acknowledge that Aboriginal and Torres Strait Islander peoples are the Traditional Custodians and the first storytellers of the lands on which we live and work. We honour Aboriginal and Torres Strait Islander peoples' continuous connection to Country, waters, skies and communities. We celebrate Aboriginal and Torres Strait Islander stories, traditions and living cultures; and we pay our respects to Elders past and present.

Powered by Penguin